2012

End or Beginning

Members of
Study Centre

MANASA FOUNDATION (R)

Taponagara, Chikkagubbi
Bangalore Urban 562149. INDIA

Phone: (080)2846 5280, 2271 5501, 93420 30250
e-mail:info@saptarishis.com
websites : www.saptarishis.com, www.lightchannels.com

2012 End or Beginning
By Study Centre

Published by

MANASA FOUDATION ®
Taponagara, Chikkagubbi
Bangalore Urban 562149. INDIA
Phone : (080)2846 5280, 2271 5501
93420 30250
e-mail : info@saptarishis.com
website : www.saptarishis.com
www.lightchannels.com

First Edition : May 2009
Second reprint : June 2009
Third reprint : August 2009
Fourth reprint : October 2009

Cover Design : Somayaji

ISBN : 978-81-88161-65-2

Rs. 100/-

Printed by
Lotus Printers Pvt. Ltd
32/25, 2nd Main Road
Sir M.V. Industrial Town
West of Chord Road, Bangalore 560 044. INDIA
Tel.: 080-2320 9909 / 2338 0167

Dedicated to the Rishis

And

Light Workers

who guide us towards Light.

Study Centre Members:

Raghavendra Somayaji

Seema Almel

Karthik C

Special Channel:

Suvahini

Channel and Guide:

Guruji Krishnananda

Contents

About the Rishis, Maharshi Amara, Guruji Krishnananda and the Special Channel Suvahini

The Rishis are the greatest souls in this Creation. They are the invisible Masters who execute the Divine Plan and guide every creature to fulfil its life's purpose. They have immense capacities to receive, hold and spread Knowledge and Wisdom.

Every soul has the potential to become a Rishi. There are many Rishis in this Creation. Most of them work under the council of Rishis known as the Hierarchy, or the Sapta Rishis, who are in charge of this earth. They monitor all the major events taking place on this earth and guide all human beings to achieve their individual and collective purpose.

Rishis are well known in the East, but the common belief is that they existed only in the past or in mythological stories, living in caves away from society, pursuing their personal Spiritual aspirations. There are many such misconceptions about them.

On the contrary, the Rishis are very real, they exist even now in the higher planes and they work selflessly for the welfare of mankind. They have enormous capacities. Their humility, Unconditional Love and Wisdom are beyond our grasp.

Currently, a team of 1,44,000 Rishis living on this earth works for the welfare of humanity under the guidance of the Hierarchy. In addition to this, there are many other Rishis from this world and higher worlds working to help humanity transform. They have access to all the Knowledge necessary for all the Ages, ranging from the Spiritual to the Material.

We are at the most crucial juncture in the Time-track of humanity. Crucial because this is the time of great changes. The Rishis play the most important role in these times by guiding us through these changes. They are waiting to help every individual to sail through these trying times and lead a life full of peace and joy.

In the present situation, the possibility of our world to be free from suffering and destruction may seem far-fetched. The Rishis say that if every individual on this earth wants peace, then all suffering will end in an instant. To begin this process, they have launched a World Movement in which, everyone *can* and *should* participate. The details of this Movement are given at the end of the book.

This book addresses the changes that this earth is going through, the reasons for these changes, their effect on us and how we can cope with them as individuals and as humanity as a whole. These guidelines are being given by the Sapta Rishis to Guruji Krishnananda and many others like him to be conveyed to everyone.

The most important contribution for this book has come from the Rishis in the form of confirmation, validation or clarification of all the New Age knowledge that was gathered and presented to them. In addition to this, new knowledge in great detail was channelled through Guruji Krishnananda.

Maharshi Amara

Maharshi Amara (1919-1982) was a very great Rishi, who spent almost his entire life working with the Sapta Rishis. A Rishi of the order of Ramana Maharshi, Ramakrishna Paramahamsa and Aurobindo, he brought down a vast amount of Knowledge from the Rishis, including the science of Meditation and interpreted it to suit the modern times. He gave the most advanced and yet simple techniques of Meditation that could be practised while leading a normal life, without going to the Himalayas or renouncing life. He initiated thousands into Meditation and guided many to their ultimate liberation.

He was not well-known during his lifetime because he deliberately kept away from publicity. He lived like any normal person and explained in simple words the concepts of Spirituality, Spiritual Pursuits, Liberation, Sanyasa, Healing, Karmas, Reincarnation and the New Age that could be understood by anyone.

He was way ahead of his times and not many could capture the essence of what he taught.

Guruji Krishnananda

One of Maharshi Amara's direct disciples, Guruji Krishnananda spent about five years in close association with him and recorded much of his teachings. Based on Maharshi Amara's teachings, he developed Dhyana Yoga and has been teaching Meditation and providing Spiritual Guidance to thousands since 1988.

Like his Guru, he shuns publicity to avoid the curious and the sundry and encourages only those who sincerely seek Spiritual guidance. He is a Light Worker and a Rishi who disseminates the Knowledge received from his Guru and the Sapta Rishis through Manasa Foundation, a non-profit and non-religious organisation founded with the sole objective of providing Spiritual guidance to seekers.

The author of several important books on Spirituality like "How to Meditate" and "Channelled Knowledge from the Rishis", his now famous book "Doorways to Light" has been regarded as the most important book after "The Autobiography of a Yogi" written by Paramahamsa Yogananda.

He has recently established a Study Centre to understand, simplify and explain Spiritual Truths to the aspirants. This book has been brought out with the combined efforts of the Study Centre and Guruji, with the most significant contributions coming from the Rishis through him.

Suvahini, The Special Channel

Suvahini is a very young lady. She had worked with the Rishis in her earlier lives. Meditations in this life have activated several of her Spiritual faculties. The Rishis are training her now for their Astral work.

Suvahini is a special channel. She can easily communicate with the Photon Belt just as she can easily communicate with the Rishis in the Astral Plane. The Knowledge she channelled for this book has enriched the content of this book.

৯৯৯

About Study Centre

The Study Centre is a centre for studies on the Spiritual Realities. Trained Meditators, under the guidance of a Master, try to gather the Knowledge about the Realities from the Rishis in the higher planes, which are beyond the grasp of the Material Science. The Rishis are reservoirs of all knowledge they have gathered directly. The knowledge channelled by the Rishis is captured by Intuition. Intuition is the main tool here.

The Study Centre, established in 2006, at "Antar-Manasa", Nadagowda Gollahalli, Bangalore Urban District by Guruji Krishnananda, is a Research wing of the Path of the Sapta Rishis established by him in 1988. Manasa Foundation (R), the organisation sustaining the activities of the Path, also teaches Meditation, as taught by the Rishis, at its headquarters at "Manasa" Taponagara, Chikkagubbi, Bangalore Urban District and various other centres. "Manasa" and "Antar-Manasa" are just a kilometre apart.

The Study Centre strives to gather the true knowledge about the Realities from the Rishis to help people remove distortions and misconceptions and improve their ways and efforts to advance into the New Age or Satya Yuga.

A Note

There is much confusion and more fear about the year 2012 in people who are familiar with the predictions for 2012. It is also true, many people are not even aware of the significance of the year 2012. This book is an attempt to explain briefly the facts and fears about 2012 and also to suggest ways to sail through it.

It is easy to scare but, it is not easy to say "Don't worry. Nothing will happen. We will be safe." The truth about 2012 is that, though many calamities are predicted by the New Agers and the Light Workers, the predictions are probabilities. They might occur or they might not. At this point of time, I can only say: "We don't know what happens." This is the truth.

Our Positivisation and Transformation impact our destiny. If we all change, the destiny changes. Then, 2012 will be a doorway to Light.

The world will not end in the year 2012. There will be a new dawn, a new beginning.

18-05-2009   —Guruji Krishnananda

Introduction

A lot has been said and written about the year 2012 in this decade alone. Much of it is available on the Internet. A simple search for '2012' fetched about 238 million web pages! And much of the content is frightening because, most sources understand it as the end of the world.

This is not the first time that a doomsday has been predicted in the history of mankind. The year 2000 is one such example from recent times, when many believed the world would come to an end. And as each such doomsday prediction fails, more and more people become sceptical about the next one, which happens to be the year 2012 at this point in time.

There are many phenomena occurring both on earth and beyond that are somehow believed to be related to the year 2012. This book, the result of research done by the *Study Centre* of Manasa Foundation, attempts to underline the importance of the year 2012 by explaining some of the phenomena. And while doing so, it also attempts to answer questions like, will the world really end or is it all just a global hoax.

To understand fully some of the phenomena that are occurring, we require deep knowledge of science, astronomy, geology etc. Since this book is aimed at providing authentic knowledge of great importance and relevance to as many people as possible, it has been written in simple English avoiding technical concepts and terms as far as possible. Wherever necessary, such concepts are explained as clearly as possible.

Interestingly, much of the phenomena related to the year 2012 are rarely reported in the mainstream media. The mainstream media seems to publish only reports that have the backing of science, meaning, phenomena explained by the mainstream science. The fact of the matter is that, many of these phenomena cannot be explained by "science" because, they are beyond the science that has been discovered by man so far.

It is important to understand that the framework of our science can only attempt to explain anything that is detectable to man and his instruments. As science advances, it succeeds in explaining more and more mysterious phenomena that could not be explained earlier.

So, the boundaries of reality as defined by science go on expanding. Therefore, the phenomena that lie outside these boundaries cannot be said to be non-existent or untrue.

To give one such example, science is unable to detect the presence of consciousness in a sentient being. Each individual *knows* that he or she is conscious and does not require proof of it.

Similarly, neither the medical science nor the judiciary is able to either detect or define the phenomenon of death with certainty (death is the permanent absence of consciousness in a being).

There have been many inconclusive medical and legal debates on this subject. In one such case, after a patient was declared brain-dead (considered to be the real confirmation of death), he became conscious, got up and walked away. (Suggested reading: "Life After Life" by Dr. Raymond Moody)

Many governments also supposedly prevent the mainstream media from reporting phenomena of global importance because, those in power believe that this may cause panic, leading to a collapse of the stock market, the economy and ultimately, the governments themselves.

This book attempts to explain phenomena that are most important and relevant today that are either beyond science or ignored by the science community. The method used in obtaining such authentic information is as follows.

First of all, the research done by this *Study Centre* is not like mainstream research where laboratories and instruments are a mainstay. Here, we try to obtain information from **highly advanced beings** who have access to all the knowledge of past, present and future.

The key 'instrument' used here to receive the knowledge is the **intuition.**

Intuition is the voice from our core, our deepest sense of self and it is never wrong. Through intuition, we can access the Source of higher wisdom.

It is very important for each individual to develop the intuition because of the very confusing times we are going through, where so many people are claiming to have authentic knowledge. If we listen to our intuition, we *will* know the truth or we will be led to the truth.

Though not widely acknowledged, intuition has played a major role in almost all the important discoveries made by modern science.

This book does not try to convince anyone or prove any theory through experimental evidence but it provides information from which the truth can be inferred by the reader.

The advanced beings mentioned above exist in a realm not yet detected by science. These beings or Masters are known in the west as angels or **Saints** and in the east as **Rishis**. Many of them lived in physical bodies like us. After they left their bodies, they chose to continue to serve or guide human beings to reduce their suffering and help them live a better life.

Though most of us have forgotten about them, the Rishis have not stopped working for our welfare. Since we cannot perceive them, they guide us through a few channels who are capable of receiving messages from them. (A channel is one who is capable of bringing down knowledge from an advanced being like a Rishi or the Higher Intelligence, the *Source* of all knowledge.)

It is indeed possible for anyone with a sharp intuition to make contact with such a Master for guidance if one is pure and selfless. The bedrock of our study work is the link with such Masters, who validate our findings and understandings.

This book is based on the work done by two channels who are in link with the Rishis. All the information provided in this book is verified by these two channels.

The first of them is Guruji Krishnananda, who has been in link with the Rishis since 1982 and has brought down an immense amount of knowledge received directly from them. Much of this knowledge has been published in the form of books and newsletter articles.

The second channel is called *Suvahini* by the Rishis (Suvahini means 'good channel' in Sanskrit). Since this channel would prefer to remain anonymous, her details are not given here. She has the amazing capacity to communicate with the Rishis, planets, stars, galaxies, energy fields, 'inanimate' objects and so on.

The information channelled by her is clearly indicated in this book and verified by Guruji Krishnananda as well. All the key points mentioned in this entire book were verified and confirmed by them in just four sessions of two hours each.

Therefore, it is important to understand that **this book is *not* just a compilation of all anecdotal information regarding 2012** available on the Internet and elsewhere.

About the Rishis and Light Workers

Science considers the birth of this universe an *accident* and that the formation of galaxies, stars, planets and the life on the planets is governed by the laws of physics and chemistry.

The truth is, there are no accidents in this universe and beyond. The Rishis and Light Workers have unimaginable powers and are the caretakers of creation and the life in the entire universe. The Higher Intelligence, the Source, the Creator of all, administers creation through them.

Though saints and Rishis are well known, what is generally not known is that they continue to work even after they leave their physical bodies.

The general perception is that this world, which is full of crooked and corrupt people, will go on exploiting the innocent forever and ever. When we are filled with such hopelessness, we must realise that the ancient Rishis and Light Workers are well aware of the situation and that they are working very hard to end the widespread injustice and suffering.

There are countless Rishis in this universe. A network of 1,44,000 Rishis is in charge of the affairs of this earth. There are many other Rishis and Light Workers supporting them. This batch of Rishis works under the guidance of the Hierarchy of seven Rishis known as the Sapta Rishis in Sanskrit. The Saptarishis work directly under the Higher Intelligence, the Source or the Creator. They have immense capacities and they guide and manage all the earths in all the galaxies of this universe.

In fact, this world has already been silently rescued several times over from various manmade and natural calamities by the Rishis. They have played an important role in the history of this world right from the birth of the amoeba. In addition to their capacities, the Rishis have enormous love, compassion and empathy for human beings and other creatures and they are trying their best to end humanity's suffering.

Structure of the book

This book is written in three parts. The first part mainly deals with the Photon Belt because it is one of most important phenomena related to the year 2012.

The second part deals with all the other phenomena expected to occur around the year 2012 such as the Galactic Alignment and the Earth Changes.

The third part, the most important, explains our role in all these events and contains clear instructions and techniques, which can be practised by anyone to sail through this interesting and eventful period.

Photon Belt

Our earth, along with the other planets in our solar system orbits around the Sun. The Sun itself revolves around a much bigger star, Alcyone, known as the Central Sun. As the Sun travels in its orbit through deep space, it encounters various fields of energy. Such fields of energy are sometimes emanations from nearby stars. These energy fields are non-physical (subtle).

Everything in creation is made up of energy. Every atom and each sub-atomic particle is made of physical (gross) energy. Every planet, star and galaxy is made up of the same energy and also has a field of subtle energy around it that influences other planets and stars.

Each energy field has its own quality and effect. For example, the energy field of our moon reaches the earth and influences all creatures on it. It is an established fact that the human mind is greatly influenced by the moon's energy field and its fluctuations.

Similarly, the other planets in our solar system and the Sun also affect and influence us in different ways and to different degrees. Even far off stars have energy fields and when we enter them, we are affected by them.

We are currently approaching the energy field of a star known as Sirius. This field of energy has many names and is commonly known as the Photon Belt.

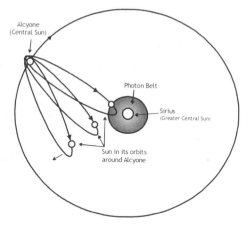

Sun in its orbits around Alcyone,
occasionally entering the energy field of Sirius

The Sirius, Alcyone and our Sun together orbit around the centre of our galaxy, the Milky way.

The Photon Belt's energy is blue in colour. Its energy is very subtle. It has intelligence like everything else in Creation. It has a very high vibratory level. A high vibratory frequency is characteristic of a higher Spiritual condition. The Photon Belt is being managed and monitored by the Saptarishis.

A spiritually evolved being like a Rishi or a saint is of a very high vibratory level. On the other hand, a self-centred and narrow minded person would have a very low vibratory level.

The implication of this is quite simple—as we get closer to the Photon Belt, we must increase our vibratory level. In other words, we need to evolve spiritually to the level of the great Rishis before the earth enters the Photon Belt.

So, some of the obvious questions that come to mind are, what do the scientists say about the Photon Belt? When are we going to enter the Photon Belt? Have we entered it before? What will happen if we do not grow spiritually by then? Is it really possible to grow to the level of the Rishis? What about those who are not aware of this?

The purpose of this book is to answer these and many other questions.

Time of Entry

Since the Photon Belt is a very subtle field of energy and not a dense physical structure like a nebula, it cannot be detected by scientists with any of their existing instruments. And even if the mainstream scientists somehow detect and confirm its existence, the governments will not allow them to make it public because of fear of causing panic.

We will be entering the Photon Belt on the **21st of December 2012** and we will be in it for a few hundred years, 505 years to be precise and not for 2000 years as it is generally believed.

On 21st December 2009, we will be entering its field of influence, meaning, the effects will begin three years before we actually enter the Photon Belt. Even before we enter its field of influence, we can connect to it and receive energies from it to accelerate our transformation.

When we enter the Photon Belt, the energies from it are first absorbed by the solar family of planets. From then onwards, their influence on earth and earthlings will change. Because of this, all astrological predictions of events after 2012 are bound to fail.

The Effects

Since the Photon Belt is a field of high frequency positive energy, anything negative on this earth cannot survive when we go through it.

Removal of all negativity from this world is a very exciting possibility for most people but not so for all! As we all know, many thrive on negativity like greed for money, power, fame etc. and would find this proposition dreadful.

For those who are innocent, selfless, honest and good, for those who are full of love, compassion, accommodation and tolerance for the fellow human being and the environment, entering the Photon Belt will be a wonderful experience because, these qualities are in tune with its vibrations.

For those who are not very good but are aware of their shortcomings and are willing to transform into a good human being, this is indeed an extremely good period. The Photon Belt creates countless opportunities for everyone to grow spiritually. In addition to creating opportunities, it also helps and accelerates our Spiritual growth like never before.

This is a great period especially for all the genuine Spiritual seekers who have been struggling to grow spiritually since many years because, very little sincere effort will bring great and quick changes when we are in or near the Photon Belt.

The Photon Belt carries a lot of Healing energies, which are required when we enter it. It can even cure diseases like cancer. The Sun receives energies from the Photon Belt, converts and passes on to us. So, we receive energies both directly from the Photon Belt and indirectly through the Sun.

The Photon Belt helps in expansion of our Consciousness. This means it helps us think and feel for others. It multiplies our faculties. It will change the human being from the worldly to the universal.

According to Suvahini, we are already receiving energies from the Photon Belt and those who are ready can receive them. Before it reaches the peak in the year 2018, we must transform completely.

Shift in Consciousness

All over the world, people have been talking about a Shift in Consciousness. This shift is being induced by many events; one of them being our entry into the Photon Belt.

The Consciousness mentioned here refers to the general pattern in the collective thinking of mankind.

All the present day systems work on the principle of barter, a system of give and take. Individuals, organizations and nations depend on such commerce for survival. All such systems are driven by fear of survival. Fear of not having enough in the future makes us resort to competition, hoarding and greed.

This is the way of the Age or Era that has now come to an end. We are entering the Age of Light. It is the Age in which there is no fear. It is the Age of abundance where commerce has no meaning. It is the Age of selflessness and oneness driven by Unconditional Love.

The Shift in Consciousness is a shift from a fear based system to the one based on love and Light. If humanity is left to itself, it will go on living in the present way and will ultimately bring destruction upon itself either through a nuclear war or by bringing about cataclysmic changes through its abuse of the environment.

When we get close to the Photon Belt, the Light from it influences everyone on this earth. It creates an explosion of awareness, which helps each individual come out of ignorance and fear and move towards new systems based on love and abundance.

Our Spiritual Growth

While we were discussing this subject, our channel, Suvahini said, "The Photon Belt will test our capacity to surrender. Tests highlight our weaknesses and give us an opportunity to recognise them and get over them. To overcome our weaknesses, we need to surrender and allow the Higher Intelligence to work through us. Without surrender, no progress is possible. In surrender, there is no fear."

What is surrender and how and what do we surrender?

Surrender is not the passive and forced submission that causes enslavement. To surrender, we must look at our negativities without any bias and humbly accept that they are there. After accepting them, we need to consciously and very clearly choose to give up those negativities.

Once we recognise, accept and choose to surrender our negativities, the energies from the Photon Belt will give us the strength required to actually give them up.

To recognise our negativities, we must understand what is Spiritual and what is not. Every human being intuitively knows what is Spiritual and what is unspiritual. It is indeed possible to make a long list of all that is unspiritual and try to recognise them in us. But there is a shorter way; an easier way to understand what is Spiritual and what is not is as follows.

Every thought, emotion and action that emanates from a person who is full of Unconditional Love will be Spiritual. With this, it is easy to understand what is not Spiritual. When a person is egoistic and full of non-love, his actions will be unspiritual.

So, to become Spiritual, we have to develop unconditional love for the fellow human being. Unconditional love does not impose any prerequisites to love someone. For example, a mother would love her children regardless of whether they are good or not, whether they are successful or not. If such love can be extended to everyone and everything, then it becomes unconditional love.

For unconditional love, the object of love is irrelevant.

It can be a friend, an animal, a tree or a rock. Such love can only emanate from a feeling of oneness towards everyone and everything.

When we enter the Photon Belt, regardless of what happens, we must fill ourselves with unconditional love and hold on to it. We should not become fearful.

All the information given in this book is not meant to induce fear; the purpose is to make the reader aware of the changes taking place and help him/her prepare and face the changes in the most appropriate way.

The Commandment

So, the only 'commandment' required to sail through the Photon Belt is to cultivate and practise unconditional love and oneness. In fact, it is not a commandment; it is only a guideline.

This will automatically increase our vibratory level to that of the Photon Belt and we can sail through it without any difficulties. What makes a Rishi or a great saint different from others is his or her unconditional love for everything in Creation *and* its Creator.

If a large number of people quickly transform globally, it can prevent or reduce much of the suffering.

Aren't the changes imposed?

What if one does not want to change? Isn't the Photon Belt an imposition on our freewill? What will happen to those who refuse to grow?

When the seasons change or calamities like earthquakes and floods occur, we accept them as natural. Some of those who believe in God may accept them as His punishment for our sins or curse Him for the destruction and suffering caused.

Just as the earth getting closer to the Sun increases the temperature and causes summer, the effects of entering the Photon Belt are natural and incidental and are not imposed. Even the suffering that results from entering the Photon Belt is not caused by the Photon Belt itself but by our resistance to positive change.

It is not mandatory for everyone to change. It does not matter whether a person is Spiritual or unspiritual. It is entirely the person's choice. There is no judgement of such choice.

In the last few thousand years, humankind has produced a large amount of negative thoughts by its collective negative thinking. All these negative thoughts, emotions and deeds have built up a huge negative field of energy around the earth.

As we enter the Photon Belt, this negative field of energy will be disintegrated by the positive vibrations of the Photon Belt because its energy field is much stronger than our collective negativity.

The destruction of the collective negative thoughts will cause upheavals at the physical level. The exact nature and extent of these physical changes depend on how all human beings prepare to enter the Photon Belt.

Relocation

Those who are very strongly attached to their possessions and refuse to give them up will be allowed to continue to have those experiences. But because of the shift in the energy field that is taking place, experiences of greed and possession will not be possible on this earth.

To allow them to have such experiences, there are seven different earths available.

As the vibratory level of our earth changes rapidly, those who cannot sustain the changes will be removed from this earth and shifted to an earth suitable to the type of life chosen by them and their Spiritual condition.

In other words, those who do not transform will **not** be judged and condemned, but will be provided worlds and opportunities where they can continue with their experiences.

But before they are shifted, they will have to leave their physical bodies and take on new ones in their new destination.

Suvahini adds, "The Photon Belt says, we have to be humble to receive the energies and gifts from it." She also says that the Photon Belt is very much hurt by our negative condition and we will be tested and rewarded if we pass them. And if we fail them, we will be shifted to earths suitable for our Spiritual condition.

She says, the Rishis are very sad because of the way we have abused and damaged Mother Earth in spite of their efforts to protect it. They, along with the Photon Belt, are healing the earth to restore it to its original splendour.

The Rishis say that from now on, we must live a life full of Light, if we don't, we will attract severe reactions. This again is not punishment, but a consequence of our actions.

If the majority of the people evolve spiritually, then the transition through the year 2012 will not be drastic at the physical level. Those who qualify will be shifted to an existence of a different frequency. They will not be visible to those who do not qualify.

The Photon Belt's energies help those who choose to live a higher life to raise their Consciousness to the highest level.

Stages of Transformation

As we approach and enter the Photon Belt, the transformation of people takes place in twelve stages as explained by Suvahini. These changes are caused by twelve different types of energies in the Photon Belt.

In the first stage, people become awakened to the reality that we need to transform in order to survive.

In the second stage, people accept and get ready for the change. They make a clear choice.

In the third stage, as a result of our choice, we face many challenges. It will be difficult to cross them. Once we surmount these challenges, we will be able to go beyond good and evil, and have contact with higher beings.

In the fourth stage, we will be able to draw higher Pranas (Vital Energy) from the Sun and live on them. We will overcome the need to eat food.

In the fifth stage, we experience oneness and we become universal beings.

In the sixth stage, many Rishis and Avatars will descend. The presence of Higher Intelligence can be felt easily.

In the seventh stage, those who have transformed spread the message, guide and help others transform.

In the eighth stage, the shift is complete with everyone's physical bodies becoming Light bodies.

In the ninth stage, everyone experiences Light.

In the tenth stage, people experience self-realisation. This is the first step to God-realisation. They become eternal and eligible to enter into the Golden Age.

In the eleventh stage, they become God. About fifty percent of the people may pass this stage.

In the twelfth stage, the Golden Age begins, and lasts for about 20,000 years. We enter the Kingdom of Oneness.

As we move from stage to stage, those who cannot make it to the next stage will be shifted out of this earth in batches.

At the end of the twelfth stage, we will be in 2018 and it will be the beginning of the Golden Age or New Age. Once we are in the New Age, we continue to have higher experiences. We continue to grow spiritually and we reach our Spiritual peak after 7000 years.

Guruji Krishnananda says, "The Rishis and Masters are already bringing the energies from the Photon Belt and distributing them to those who are ready. Many are struggling to receive, accept and cope-up with the energies. We struggle because we doubt.

"Complete transformation or metamorphosis involves a replacement of the old with the new, like the butterfly emerging from its cocoon."

Effect on Time

The Dark Age, which we have been going through for the last five thousand years has ended in 1974. Since then, we are in the transitory period—a period of transition from the Dark Age or Kali Yuga to the Light Age or Satya Yuga or the New Age.

The duration of the transitory period is normally 432 years, during which the people of this world get the opportunities to transform and adapt to the new ways of the Light Age at a normal pace.

The Light Age or the New Age is a period in which darkness cannot exist. It is a period full of Light, love and abundance. It is a period when people live a perfect life full of bliss and harmony with no fear, disease or suffering of any kind.

For many, it is difficult to believe the possibility of such perfect conditions, given the current state of affairs. However, the Golden Age is not an utopian fantasy and the earth *will* enter it regardless of the present conditions.

The Light Age will last for 20,304 years and after that, the Spiritual condition of people will begin to degenerate. This degeneration continues for the next three periods of darkness of 15,228 years, 10,152 years and 5,076 years, with the negativity at its peak during the last five thousand years.

These Ages are cyclic and we enter the Light Age once again after the transitory period. (For detailed information, please read the chapter 'Time and its Cycles' in the book "*New Age Realities*" by the Study Centre.)

Many do not agree with these numbers. Some believe that the Kali Yuga will go on for hundreds of thousands of years. The accurate information regarding the Ages has been lost during one of the previous upheavals. These numbers were given by Guruji Krishnananda's Guru, Maharshi Amara, who was a very great Rishi with direct access to the Source of all knowledge.

The earth has been through such cycles many times and in each cycle, there can be variations in the way we go through the transitory periods. One of the influencing factors is the Photon Belt.

According to Suvahini, we may enter the Photon Belt several times in each cycle or we may not enter it at all. In this cycle of 51,840 years, we have been through it 108 times.

Time itself moves faster when we enter the Photon Belt. By its influence, the transitory period of 432 years from the Dark Age to the Light Age will be reduced to just 44 years. This means that the New Age will begin fully in the year 2018.

The Photon Belt says, contrary to general belief, our day of twenty four hours actually takes only fourteen hours. The Photon Belt will reduce it further to twelve hours a day. In November 2010, it will be ten hours a day.

This involves many great and rapid changes, both in the individuals and the earth, and will be spread over seven years beginning from the year 2012. Because of the increasing pace of changes, it is difficult for many people to change and adapt quickly. But during this period, maximum opportunities and maximum possible help comes from the Photon Belt, the Rishis and Avatars.

According to Suvahini, in one of the past cycles, the Light Age began in 2032. If we do not encounter the Photon Belt, we will have a longer period of 432 years to transform. She says, the Photon Belt has become very active from 20th April 2009, 8:50pm.

In any case, the Photon Belt makes our entry into Light Age faster, skipping many painful experiences.

What next?

Even if all of this is not true, all we are saying here is to develop unconditional love and oneness. Even if the photon belt is not a reality, if a large number of people can practise these two things, then this world will be a better place to live in. Because of the collective positive thought force, much of the negativity can be nullified.

How do we prepare to enter the Photon Belt without suffering? For an answer to this question, please read the chapter titled *"Action Plan"* at the end of this book.

It was 1pm on 21st April 2009 and we finished our discussion on the Photon Belt. We were in a dazed state. When we stepped out of the Study Centre, everything looked different. But life was going on as usual.

The mindless traffic, the rat-race for survival in offices, schools and businesses, governments speculating that the world will soon come out of economic recession, the stock markets back to their speculative buying and selling, the corrupt politicians vying to return to power so that they may rule the country for five more years ...

Everything outside seemed to go on in a 'normal' way, as if it could go on and on, ad infinitum.

When we look at the world outside, it is difficult to believe that all of this has to change in a matter of two years. Yes, it is very difficult to accept. But the truth does not depend on our beliefs. The truth is what it is.

Those who find it hard to believe this should sharpen their intuition, try to feel the change in the energies around and follow the global events taking place. Soon, The Shift will become self-evident.

We are reminded of the story of Lot from the Bible, where he is warned by the angels to leave the city of Sodom before it is destroyed. He tries in vain to convince the others that the city will be destroyed and they must flee to save their lives, which of course, no one believes ...

The Year 2012

Before we go into the details of other events expected to occur in the year 2012, it is important to understand that these are not ominous events but are so positive and good that they are worth celebrating. By the time we reach the end of this book, we expect the reader to be excited and looking forward to the year 2012.

Many events are expected to occur in the year 2012. One of the most important events being the entry of our earth and the solar system into the Photon Belt, which has been explained in detail in the previous section.

This section explains some of the other equally important events that are expected to occur between the year 2012 and 2018. The year 2018 is when all the changes and effects culminate.

As explained in the previous section, because of our proximity with the Photon Belt, its influence will begin three years earlier—from 21st December 2009. The next major event is the alignment of our Sun with the centre of our galaxy, which coincides with our entry into the Photon Belt. This of course, is not a coincidence.

Our Galaxy

First, a brief background.

Our earth along with the other planets in our solar system orbit around the Sun. The Sun orbits around a much larger star known as Alcyone or the Central Sun. Alcyone in turn revolves around a massive star known as Sirius, also called the Greater Central Sun.

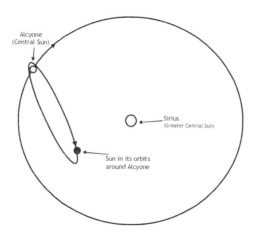

The Sun and Alcyone in their orbits

This revolution of one star around another continues to many levels. Ultimately, all the stars in the entire galaxy spin around the centre of the galaxy. Our galaxy, the Milky Way has an estimated 300 billion stars.

The Milky Way

What makes 300 billion stars spin around a central point at high speeds? What could be the extent of gravity at the centre of the galaxy?

It is difficult to imagine the immense mass and gravity of the Galactic Centre. At the centre of each galaxy, there is a super-massive white hole or black hole that has enough gravity to make the entire galaxy go around it. (For more information on Black Holes, please read the book *New Age Realities* by the Study Centre.)

The Universe has billions of small and large galaxies.

The significance of this hierarchy of stars in the galaxy is as follows:

We receive higher Spiritual energies from the stars. For example, the energies we receive from Alcyone are higher than those we receive from our Sun. Similarly, the energies we receive from Sirius are of a higher order than those we receive from Alcyone and so on.

The most powerful Spiritual vibrations therefore, emanate from the Galactic Centre, both directly and through the Sun and the Central Sun.

We receive energies from all the stars and the Galactic Centre all the time. But we normally receive them in small quantities. In order to receive the maximum amount of energies, our earth must come in proper alignment with the source of the energy.

For example, when the earth, the Sun and the moon fall in a straight line, we receive the maximum amount of energies from the Sun. Such an alignment causes an eclipse during which we can receive and absorb more energies by meditating to boost our Spiritual growth.

During eclipses, the earth receives more energies. These energies have a positive influence on nations and peoples. They sometimes influence global events. There are many myths and beliefs about the effects of eclipses. In some countries, people do not venture out during a solar eclipse and after the eclipse, they take a bath to wash off the "ill effects". This is a distortion of facts.

The ancients knew about the benefits of the energies received during eclipses. They stayed indoors not out of fear, but to meditate and receive the maximum amount of energies from the Sun. And after the eclipse, they would take a bath to wash off the excess energies deposited on their bodies.

During an eclipse, many types of energies are released. There are many Rishis who are experts in this field. During each eclipse, they harvest these energies and store them on earth or elsewhere, to be used when humanity requires them. They also send these energies to everyone on this earth during the eclipse to help their Spiritual growth and awakening.

Each eclipse takes us a step closer to the Light Age.

Similarly, when the Sun comes in alignment with the Central Sun and the Greater Central Sun, we receive higher energies that advance our Spiritual growth. This alignment occurs not in a straight line but in a triangle on a plane.

The three suns in alignment

This event is expected to occur in the year 2012. The energies from these stars bring about many positive global changes.

Celestial Intelligence

The celestial bodies like the earth, the Sun and the stars are not lifeless objects traversing through the universe. Everything in creation has intelligence. Even a "lifeless" stone has intelligence in it.

All matter, physical or non-physical, is made from a very fundamental Divine Matter known as Consciousness. The underlying Consciousness of everything in creation is the same. A stone is a form taken by Consciousness.

Similarly, a tree, an animal and a human being are all forms taken by the same underlying Consciousness. Consciousness itself is formless. Because of this, everything in creation is interconnected; everything in creation is *one*.

All Consciousness has awareness and intelligence. The core of any such field of intelligence has a personality with which we can communicate.

Such a core or a Divine Personality exists for the energy fields of the earth, the moon, the Sun, the Stars and the Galactic Centre. The Divine personality of the earth is commonly known as Mother Earth or Gaia (*Bhoodevi* in Sanskrit). The personality of the Sun in some cultures is known as RA, the Sun God (*Suryanarayana* in Sanskrit).

The Galactic Centre also has a Divine Personality at its core (*Pranava Purusha* in Sanskrit). A hierarchy exists between these Divine Personalities and goes all the way up to the Source. Their primary purpose is to create and sustain life in planets like the earth. The Rishis and Light Workers work with these personalities for the welfare of all life on all the earths.

The energies we receive during the celestial alignments are from these Divine Personalities and therefore, are very sacred and very important for our Spiritual evolution.

Galactic Alignment

As the Sun orbits the Central Sun, it also goes around the Galactic Centre. It takes millions of years to complete one orbit. Seen from the galactic plane, the Sun traverses around the Galactic Centre, not in a straight line but in a waveform like a merry-go-round.

Movement of the Sun along the Galactic Plane

When the Sun touches the Galactic Plane, it is said to be in alignment with the Galactic Centre. This alignment happens once in thousands of years. When the Sun is in alignment with the Galactic Centre, energies of a very high vibratory level flood the earth and our solar system. The effects of these energies are explained later.

Interestingly, this alignment is expected to occur on the 21st of December 2012, when the earth enters the Photon Belt. The combined effect of these two events will be massive from a Spiritual point of view. The two events occurring on exactly the same day is not a coincidence. It is a part of the Divine Plan and it is to help humanity evolve quickly without very great effort.

As with all events, the date of alignment of our solar system with the Galactic Plane is a subject of debate across various groups. It is believed by some groups that the Sun came in alignment with the Galactic Centre in 1980 and it will take 36 years to move across the thickness of the Galactic Centre.

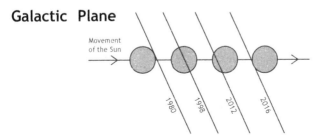

Movement of the Sun along the Galactic Plane

This means that the alignment with the centre of the galaxy must have occurred in the year 1998 and that we will be completely out of alignment with the Galactic Centre in the year 2016.

There are other estimates for the time of the Sun's alignment with the Galactic Centre, such as the period between 1982 and 2018.

The thickness of the Galactic Centre is **estimated** to be one thousand light years. It is virtually impossible to know the exact boundaries of the Galactic Centre from the earth, which is **estimated** to be between 24,600 to 27,400 light years away. Therefore it is possible that the actual alignment may happen a few years before or after these dates.

One of the effects of the Photon Belt is the compression of Time and Space. Because of this, the exact time of alignment arrived at by using conventional methods is unlikely to be accurate, since the rate of compression of time is not fixed and unknown.

How can we know the exact date and time of such an alignment and why is it so important?

One of our Meditators had an experience. Before she had this experience, she did not know about the time of Galactic Alignment. A part of that experience is quoted here:

"After we were told that we could talk to the Photon Belt, I requested the Photon Belt to speak to me. The Photon Belt said the following to me.

"'On 21st December 2012, at 11:11am Universal Time, the earth, the Suns and the Galactic Centre will be in an alignment. This will have a powerful effect, which will cause the reversal of the magnetic axis of the Sun and the earth. It is the wish of the Prime Creator that the Galactic Alignment takes place at the same time as the earth enters me'.

"The Photon Belt then told me, 'Make yourself pure, keep yourself open. I am here to help you, I am here to uplift your

Consciousness.' The Photon Belt then passed me blue coloured energies.

"After the experience, I searched on the Internet for information on 2012 and I was surprised to find the same date and time there."

Effects of Galactic Alignment

The effects of the Galactic Alignment combined with the entry into the Photon Belt can be grouped into two as physical and Spiritual. While the Galactic Alignment brings about both physical and Spiritual changes, the Photon Belt's influence is purely Spiritual.

Earth Changes

As the force of earth's magnetic field is maximum at the equator, the force of the Galactic Centre's magnetic field is maximum at the Galactic Plane. When the Sun and the earth enter the zone of the galactic plane, there will be a disruption of their magnetic fields.

For a brief period, the magnetic poles may disappear and then reappear at different locations later, they are today. This will affect the earth's geographical poles also.

At present, the earth is tilted at a certain angle on its axis. As a result of the Galactic Alignment, the earth's tilt may change by several degrees. This shift of geographic poles will result in a shift of the ice caps at the poles.

At the time of entering the galactic plane, which is 21st December 2012, 11:11am Universal Time, the rotation of the earth may stop for three days or nights, depending on where we are at that time. After that the earth will begin to rotate again in the opposite (clockwise) direction.

According to Suvahini, on 21st December 2012, when the earth stops rotating, there will be earthquakes, eruptions of volcanoes, cyclones etc. These changes are caused by Galactic Alignment and not because of the Photon Belt.

However, these changes will not affect the people who have accepted and transformed. While some of these changes are initiated by the earth to heal herself, others are caused by the collective negativity of mankind.

While discussing these points, Suvahini said, "Yesterday (19th April 2009), the geographic pole shifted by half a degree and the magnetic pole shifted by one degree. The Rishis energised and stabilised the Photon Belt yesterday. They attached millions of lights to it to strengthen it so that the transformation is quick. Photon Belt is receiving blue and pink energies from the Source. These energies correspond to strength and healing respectively."

She added, "The magnetic poles shifted by 1 degree on 9th April 2009. The total shift will be 20 to 30 degrees by 2018, depending on the extent of humanity's transformation. The Magnetic pole shift promotes goodness, evil becomes less effective, our cells undergo changes that enable them to hold more Light and the Kundalini can rise easily."

She continued, "The magnetic grid is changing *right now* by 1.5 degrees ... it is now 8.5 degrees (22nd April 2009).

There will be one more shift during the next solar eclipse, which is on 22nd July 2009. The possibility of geographic pole shift is about 60% now."

The magnetic grid is a network of magnetic lines of force that criss-cross the planet. Among other things, the magnetic grid is used by migratory fish and birds for navigation.

The shifting of geographic poles and the occurrence of all major events is determined by the collective Spiritual condition of the people living on earth at that time. If people transform quickly, a shift in the collective Consciousness will prevent any cataclysmic changes on earth.

Suvahini says, the magnetic pole shift can bring about transformation in 95% of the people. It removes pettiness and will help them to surrender their shortcomings instantly.

The earth *has* changed its direction of rotation in the past several times and it has been recorded by the geologists. The tilt of the earth is already changing, causing the poles to drift. This shift of the polar regions is what is causing the polar ice to melt and not global warming caused by greenhouse gases as it is generally understood.

As we shall witness in the not so far off future, all polar ice will melt, submerging all land at sea level until the ice is relocated to the new poles.

The Sun's magnetic poles have already disappeared. This will have an impact on the earth's magnetic as well as geographic poles.

Mother earth or Gaia is aware of these changes. She knows when to initiate them and renew herself. She is also guided by the Rishis and Light Workers.

Interestingly, it was recently reported that the trees have begun to absorb more carbon dioxide from the atmosphere than they used to because of the increased availability of CO_2, there by reducing the greenhouse effect.

Also, scientists have noticed that while global warming has actually stopped since the year 2001[1], the rise in temperature has been higher at the poles than in rest of the world[2].

Since the year 2003, the oceans have actually cooled[3]. Across the world, there have been reports of unseasonal snow, dropping temperatures and snowstorms[4], with China experiencing its coldest winter in the last hundred years[5] and Germany's temperature dropping to -28 degrees Celsius while the polar ice caps continue to melt unabated at alarming rates.

Many people *have* actually noticed a shift in the magnetic poles already with the help of the ordinary compass[6] and satellite images. Former vice president of the United States and Nobel laureate, Mr. Al Gore, who has been a champion of global warming and weather changes has documented many of the recent climate changes in his film "The Inconvenient Truth".

1 dsc.discovery.com/news/2009/03/02/global-warming-pause.html
2 www.sciencedaily.com/releases/2009/01/090121144049.html
3 www.theaustralian.news.com.au/story/0,25197,24122117-7583,00.html
4 www.telegraph.co.uk/comment/columnists/christopherbooker/3563532/The-world-has-never-seen-such-freezing-heat.html
5 www.dailytech.com/Temperature+Monitors+Report+Worldwide+Global+Cooling/article10866.html
6 www.rense.com/general51/mag.html

The shift of the geographic poles has been referred to in the Bible and recorded in the cultures of Egypt, Hopi and Pawnee Indians, Eskimos, Chinese to name a few.

Collapse of man-made systems

As a result of the powerful magnetic radiation from the Galactic Centre, all electric and electronic devices will fail. All power stations will fail to produce electricity. This can have far reaching effects.

Those who hold on to their negativities through attachment and greed will suffer when they lose their prized possessions. Humanity will be tested with the collapse of many man-made systems that are essential to today's way of life. We will be jolted out of our indifference through these collapses.

One such collapse we have seen recently is the collapse of our economy. As we move towards a period of truth, all that is false *must* and *will* collapse.

With the disruption of power stations and all that works on electromagnetism, all forms of communication that require electricity like radio, television, telephones, mobile phones, e-mail and Internet will stop working. Even the print media will not be able to print newspapers without electricity. All modes of transportation that use some technology will fail leading to disruption of all supply chains.

This leads to total isolation. People will not be able to communicate with each other or travel. This means, all governments will collapse as it is impossible to run a country without communication. When all means of transportation fail, even essential commodities like food and medicines cannot be made available.

All other systems like the medical industry, the air force, army, navy, police etc. will stop functioning because all technology requires electricity. Normal life will be completely affected. One may wonder how can anyone survive in such a situation.

Surviving the Collapses

It is obvious that it will not be possible to survive in such conditions with the means available today. Such conditions may lead to looting and anarchy for some time but soon, all hoardings of supplies will be exhausted and people will have nothing to loot or fight over.

Before all this happens, many people all over the world will practise certain principles and techniques that not only help them evolve spiritually but also physically. Their cells undergo certain changes that will make them less dependent on food.

They will be able to absorb Prana, the Vital Energy from the Sun, and convert it into glucose required by the cells initially. There are already people who can survive entirely on Prana. As the Spiritual evolution continues, the physical body transforms completely into a Light body, which draws sustenance from the Sun.

A Light body, though physical, is far subtler than the present biological body. Since it vibrates at a higher level, it is less dense and therefore it will not be affected by any of the physical disturbances. Even a nuclear explosion cannot affect a Light body.

For some time both people with physical bodies and Light bodies will remain in the same realm while those in Light bodies try to help the others to transform. Electricity will be replaced by a new form of energy that can be drawn directly from the atmosphere. Each household will be able to generate it and also manifest anything that is required. There will be no central authority to control the supply of energy. There will be no business, commerce, police etc.

Guruji Krishnananda says, "When a human system fails, it will be replaced with a Divine system. When communication fails, it can be done through thoughts. When no food is available, we learn to receive energies directly from the Sun. We survive and develop new systems. Life goes on."

He continues, "There are Light beings, Astral Masters and a Divine plan waiting to help us and gift us with higher living facilities and comforts. We have to get ready to receive them. We have to qualify to receive them. How do we qualify? We can qualify by just going back to our original state: the state of Love, Peace and Truth. Positivise, remove all violence, corruption and aggression. It is not easy but we have not tried it. We have to meditate and channel Light a lot to transform. It *is* actually possible for the transition into the Light Age to be peaceful and painless."

Those with a Light body will develop special capabilities. They will be able to communicate with others in Light bodies telepathically. They will also be able to communicate with the Rishis and Light Workers, who will guide them through these upheavals.

As time passes, those with Light bodies find themselves in a different realm, where they find everything transformed and beautiful.

To quote from the Bible, *"Ye shall be changed to immortality in the twinkling of an eye."*

Bodily Changes

The powerful vibrations emanating from the Photon Belt and the energies from the Galactic Centre, though subtle, also influence our physical bodies. The bodily changes that occur help us in growing spiritually. As these changes occur, it becomes easier for us to choose the ways of the Light Age approaching us.

The importance of the physical body has been ignored by many Spiritual seekers. It imposes a very strong influence on our personality. The body and the mind influence and complement each other. For example, a feeling such as fear can be felt in the body as increased heart rate, sweating etc. Similarly, a wound in the body causes pain, which is felt in the mind.

All the thoughts from the intellect and emotions from the mind have an impact on the physical body. Very strong and long standing negative thoughts and emotions bring about permanent changes in the body. Their energies get transferred to the cells and get strengthened if such thoughts and emotions persist. They ultimately become a part of the personality and manifest at the physical level as diseases etc.

To remove the effects of these thoughts and emotions, it is not enough to make changes in our mind and intellect, which is relatively easy. If a person stops thinking negatively and avoids negative emotions, they bring about changes in the intellect and the mind but not as quickly in the body. For these changes to be reflected in the physical body takes much longer.

For example, recently, a person with a damaged heart underwent a heart transplantation. Soon after he recovered from the surgery, he developed an urge to smoke, a desire which he never had before the surgery. Later, it was found out that the donor of the heart was a heavy smoker and that his craving was transferred to the recipient through the heart's tissues.

The energies from the Photon Belt, the Galactic Centre and the changes in the earth's magnetic field make it far easier to dissolve such negative impressions in our tissues. The changes must occur at the cellular level if we are to grow spiritually. This is why, transforming the physical body is so important.

As we continue to receive these energies and the Prana (Vital Energy) from the Sun, our tissues undergo certain changes that make them less dependent on energy derived from food. These energies, combined with long Meditations bring about changes at the cellular level. We will be able to completely live on Prana alone, without the need to consume food and water. This will render the digestive system rudimentary. The Pineal gland, located behind the Pituitary gland develops and increases its capacity to absorb more Prana and Light.

By the year 2012, if we have absorbed enough Pranas and energies through regular and long Meditations, our bodies will be completely transformed into Light bodies.

Guruji Krishnananda says, "It is indeed possible to get rid of all traces of negativity in an instant by throwing away all our baggage. Without the energies from the Photon Belt and the Galactic Centre, it would be far more difficult to transform, requiring longer hours of Meditation and more effort."

Suvahini says, "The Light we are currently receiving brings about changes in everyone's Chakras and the Kundalini energy. This will help us absorb more Light and transform faster."

Pranas and Nadis

Our physical body and Astral body are glued to each other by the Vital Body. (The Astral body is the combined sheaths of the mind, intellect and the causal body.) Prana, the energies from the Sun (Spiritual) and the moon (material), flows through a network of channels in the Vital body (*Nadis* in Sanskrit).

As the earth undergoes geographic changes, its gravity becomes weaker and weaker. Ultimately, when it stops rotating, the gravity becomes so weak that the moon, which is currently in the grip of earth's gravity, slips away and drifts into the solar system.

With the absence of the moon, fluctuations of the mind will stop. There will be no agitations. The capacity of the mind increases and new faculties become active.

As the moon drifts away, we stop receiving energies from it.

This upsets the system of channels of Prana in the vital body. These channels will soon be flooded with energies from the Second Sun to restore the balance (Second Sun is described later in this section). In the absence of the moon, the conditions will not be suitable for pure materialism.

With the absence of material energies from the moon and presence of Spiritual energy of a very high order from the Second Sun, those who accept these energies will transform into Light beings.

Kundalini of the 34th type will rise and fill up the entire system. Currently, a Kundalini energy of a type between seven and twelve will be active. By the year 2018, the 72nd Kundalini, the highest, will be active in those who have transformed. These energies burn our Karmas very fast.

Since the frequency of a Light body is much higher than that of the physical body, those in Light bodies will be invisible. Billions of such people in Light bodies will be shifted to a different, subtler realm. Those who are unable to transform will continue to live in their physical bodies.

This new realm will exist in the same space and those in physical bodies will not be aware of the new realm. This is comparable to the city of Shambala, which currently exists on this earth but in a different realm, making it inaccessible to ordinary human beings.

Shambala

Shambala is a city of Light located somewhere in the Gobi desert, accessible only to the Rishis and advanced beings.

During each Light Age, this city will be open to everyone. After the Light Age ends and the next Age begins, the Spiritual condition of man begins to degenerate. When this happens, the city of Shambala will be closed again, allowing only those who retain their advanced Spiritual state.

As the degeneration continues and the vibratory level of man reduces significantly, Shambala becomes invisible, since it vibrates at a higher frequency.

If an individual wants to see or visit the City of Shambala, he/she has to increase their vibratory level by improving their Spiritual condition.

When the shift in Consciousness occurs in the year 2012, those who choose the higher Consciousness will enter a state similar to that of Shambala. Those who are unable to choose the higher Consciousness, continue to exist in the realm that we are in now. (For more information on Shambala, please read 'Doorways to Light' by Guruji Krishnananda.)

Arrival of the World Teacher

Most major religions of the world believe that their founder will return to save the world. While Christians believe in the return of the Christ, Buddhists believe that Buddha will reincarnate as Maitreya. The Jews await the return of the Messiah, the Muslims await the Imam Mahdi and the Hindus await the tenth incarnation of Vishnu known as Kalki.

Regardless of the name used, they all refer to the same World Teacher, who is already actively managing the Shift in Consciousness. He was born in 1924 in Shambala and since then

He has been preparing, working and waiting to intensify the transformation process. He lives in Shambala.

Suvahini adds, "Lord Kalki says, His activities will peak in the year 2012 since the conditions created by the Photon Belt, the Galactic Alignment, the magnetic pole shifts and other events will create an ideal condition for transformation through His action. In the year 2012, He will employ Light to remove impurity from humanity. Many will not withstand the purification process."

She continues, "The effects begin in January 2012 and peak on 21st December 2012. I can see a lot of chaos."

Judgement Day

Some religions speak of the *Day of Judgment* when God or His representatives descend from the heavens and judge how each individual has lived on this earth. This is not a single day of judgement but a period from the year 2012 to 2018, the *seven years of tribulation* mentioned in the Bible.

But no one will sit in judgement and judge anyone. Instead, the pure energies flooding the earth during this period will, as a natural process remove impurity from everyone.

Many will continue to live without any transformation because that is what they choose.

Guruji Krishnananda says, "This is also a kind of payback time. The Universe is ready to pay back. It will pay back for whatever it has received from us. If we have been sending only positive vibrations, the Universe will send back the same in multiples. Our emotions, both positive and negative, reach the Universe.

"It is the duty of the Universe to pay back. This is not punishment. It is an opportunity to realize our mistakes and correct ourselves. It is a time of instant forgiveness. If we genuinely accept our mistakes and regret, we are forgiven. There will be no more Karmas, problems or sufferings."

Other 2012 Events

This section lists some other important events that are expected in the year 2012.

Second Sun

All the stars that have life on one of their planets have a companion star or a twin star. Our Sun also has its twin, known as the Second Sun (*Dwitiya Suryanarayana* in Sanskrit). The Second Sun is not visible like the Sun. It exists at a subtler level like Shambala but it can become physical if necessary.

The Second Sun is wrongly believed to be a distant planet or a brown dwarf star by many astronomers and New Agers and is known by names like Planet X, Nibiru, Nemesis and so on.

The Second Sun is not a planet or a dead star but a real star that is behind the Sun when seen from the earth. Sometimes it is visible to spiritually evolved individuals. And when it is visible, it is blindingly bright.

The Second Sun's energies are blue in colour. It is very bright and much bigger than our Sun.

Photograph of both Suns taken at sunset on January 2002
by Ms. Soluntra King at Pilot Bay Mt. Maunaganui, New Zealand.

The above photograph was taken by the Light worker Ms. Soluntra King in New Zealand. Many Light workers worked very hard to make the Second Sun visible so that it could be photographed.

The Second Sun does not revolve around the Sun and it does not have its own planets. The distance between the two Suns is constant. Whenever the Sun is weak, the Second Sun acts as a backup and supplements the Sun with its energies.

The Second Sun is playing a major role now. The energies released from the Second Sun will increase in 2012 to help the transition. We have to receive Prana (Vital Energy) from the Second Sun in order to transform. Our Nadis (Pranic Network in our Vital Body) are already changing to receive higher Prana from the Second Sun.

When we are unable to come out of the darkness, we take the help of the Second Sun. The Rishis know when to activate the Second Sun and when not to. The Second Sun is waiting to contact us. Henceforth, we have to begin interacting with the Second Sun.

The energies from the Second Sun help us to open up to newer realities. The Second Sun is a source of advanced knowledge that will be required in the Light Age.

Mayans

The Mayans who lived in Central America during 2000 BC were very advanced beings. They were experts in mathematics and astronomy. With their knowledge, they charted many calendars. The Mayan Calendar not only helps in measuring days, months and years and longer periods of time but also indicates different phases in the Spiritual evolution of human beings.

Their 'Long Count' calendar, which is approximately 5126 years of the Gregorian calendar, ends on 21st December 2012 and a new one begins i.e., it resets from 12.19.19.17.19 to 13.0.0.0.0.

Whenever the long count calendar ends, a phase in the Spiritual evolution of man ends and a new phase begins. As it is generally believed, the end of the Mayan calendar does not indicate the end of the world. It indicates the beginning of a New Age, a new era.

Their calendars are far more advanced and accurate when compared to the presently used Gregorian calendar, which has many flaws.

The Mayans were aware of the Sun's orbit around the galaxy and the frequency and importance of its alignment with the Galactic Centre. It is believed that their long count calendar resets on 21st December 2012 because of the Galactic Alignment and restarts to indicate a new phase in the life of people on earth. The Mayans believed that an alignment with the Galactic Centre also implied an 'alignment' or tuning with the Higher Intelligence.

Guruji Krishnananda says, "The Mayans did not study nor research to gain knowledge. They had such knowledge even before they came to this earth. They came from a star which is near the centre of our galaxy.

"The Mayans tried to give their knowledge to the people of this earth but no one was interested or ready for it. They tried to help reduce the suffering of humanity. They were in touch with the Rishis. The Rishis asked them to return to their planet. There are many theories about their sudden disappearance. They left in their physical bodies in spaceships. They will return to earth after some time."

Ms. Soluntra King, a Light worker from New Zealand, once had an experience in which the Mayan Calendar spoke to her. It said that the earth will be entering the field of influence of the Photon Belt on 21st December 2009, giving us a three year period from then onwards for our preparation.

Galactic Cycle

Our Central Sun, Alcyone, revolves around the centre of the galaxy, taking 225 million years to complete one orbit. Alcyone's galactic cycle also ends in the year 2012 and is considered to be significant.

Solar Cycles

Sunspots are planet sized dark patches on the Sun with intense magnetic activity that reduces the region's temperature and brightness. The appearance of sunspots is cyclic and their periodicity is approximately eleven years, which constitutes a Solar Cycle.

Due to intense magnetic activity during a solar cycle, solar flares erupt. A solar flare is a giant explosion on the Sun's surface with such intensity that the X-Rays and Ultraviolet Rays emitted by them reach the earth, disrupting radio communication and power grids.

The current solar cycle is expected to end around 2012. Satellite operators and space mission planners are bracing for the next solar cycle because it is expected to be exceptionally stormy and may cause earthquakes, eruption of volcanoes and floods.

A solar flare that reaches the earth carries energies for our transformation. All the planets are aware of these changes.

The Age of Aquarius

In astrology, as the Sun travels in space, it passes through twelve star constellations known as the Zodiac. At present we are said to be passing through Pisces and we are expected to enter the Aquarius soon. This is considered important because the Aquarian Age is seen as synonymous with the Golden Age.

But the exact date of entry into Aquarius is not known. While some say that we are already in it, others say that we will be entering Aquarius after 360 years.

Suvahini says, "We have already entered the Aquarian Age and we are presently receiving energies from Aquarius, which are bluish white in colour. Aquarius is saying that by entering it, a lot of confusion will be created among people, which helps them absorb more Light and move towards their higher self faster."

Guruji Krishnananda says, "Each constellation is a field of energy that influences us. The main influence of entering Aquarius is that it causes the true nature of individuals to surface so that they can face it and deal with it. Some mistakes made in the past life also surface. This is an opportunity given to accept them."

He continues, "Each Zodiac has all the twelve types of energies and has its own special energy. Since we are entering the Photon Belt, the energies required for transformation are being invoked, which is why Suvahini could see blue energies. In fact, any Zodiac sign could have released these energies. The influence of Aquarius is minute when compared with the influence of the Photon Belt."

Schumann Resonance

When global electromagnetic waves pass through the space between the earth's surface and the upper part of the atmosphere, they resonate at a certain frequency. This is known as the Schumann Resonance. They normally occur at a frequency of 7.8 cycles per second. The frequency can vary in different locations, under different conditions.

This resonance is commonly known as the earth's heartbeat or Gaia's heartbeat.

The importance of Schumann Resonance came to light when astronauts spending extended periods of time in outer space experienced distress and disorientation. When a device to artificially generate the Schumann Waves was installed in the spacecraft, the space sickness disappeared. (www.luxevivant.com/index.asp?pageAction=Custom&ID=68)

Therefore, to live a normal life, the Schumann Waves are essential.

Recent measurements indicate that the Schumann Resonance has increased to 11 cycles per second.

According to Suvahini, the Schumann Resonance is now at 11.34 Hertz. It is expected to rise gradually to 15 Hertz. towards the end of the transitory period, which is 2018. At this frequency, negativity in us cannot survive. The Schumann Resonance will reach a maximum of 22.82 Hertz at the peak of the Golden Age.

She says, when Gaia's heartbeat increases, it helps bring out suppressed negativity. After that the individual has to deal with it. The increased frequency also helps us hear the voice of the Light and adjust to its frequency and to adjust to higher Pranic energies. This helps us to receive Pranas directly from the Second Sun.

Predictions

There have been a few seers and prophets like Nostradamus,

Merlin The Wild and Mother Shipton, who have quite accurately predicted some major world events, have also spoken about great changes around the year 2012. There are books like the Chinese I-Ching or 'The Book of Changes' and the Bible that make predictions about such world events.

There is one modern day 'prophet' that has baffled even scientists. It is a complex computer software that works with millions of smaller programs that work through the Internet to gather data from conversations between people. It was originally meant to analyse this data to gauge the trends in the collective human thinking so that it may lead to clues about the trends in the stock market.

Though it was designed to make predictions for the financial markets, its users observed that the future events that could cause emotional disturbances in people were also being predicted. Somehow, people are collectively becoming aware of future disasters.

Some of the predictions made by this software are, the attack on the twin towers in September 2001 in New York (prediction made in June 2001), the tsunami of 2004, anthrax attack on Washington and many others.

Its next major predictions are, a nuclear war or equivalent in 2008 or 2009 and a series of catastrophes that will peak in a global event towards the end of 2012 (urbansurvival.com/simplebots.htm).

Life after 2012

In spite of all the information available with us, it is difficult to imagine what life would be like after the year 2012. Here, we provide some more details and experiences that may help in that direction.

All those who survive 2012 can be grouped into two: those who have begun transforming and those who have not. The reality perceived by them depends entirely on their inner Spiritual condition.

Guruji Krishnananda says, "The Rishis and masters in the Astral plane come in contact with us to guide us. We have to develop contact with them so that we can receive guidance from them. Such guidance is a must during 2012. Which is why we, from now onwards, have to do longer Meditations and go on trying to talk to the Light."

The extent of transformation and the number of people who transform determines events like pole shifts and other earth changes. Even the availability of electricity depends on the extent of global transformation.

People become vegetarians. Hence the killing of animals for food will stop. People stop using artificial materials like plastics that harm the environment. They switch to natural materials like cotton. Consumption of alcohol stops.

People who are still dependent on food will learn to take in more Prana from the Sun and the Second Sun. It will be some time before they can start living entirely on Prana.

Everyone will be healthy with their bodies proportionate in size. There will be no thin or fat people.

Electricity will be replaced with a different kind of energy, which can be drawn from the atmosphere. Each household will have their own source of infinite and free power, with no need to depend on a central power grid.

There will be new species of life that can experience more, with higher awareness. Even a stone will have higher vibrations.

Everything on earth, every atom absorbs more Light and shines with Divine Light. We enter into a new Consciousness, which is based on Love.

A Meditator, known for her amazing visions and experiences, had a vivid dream in which it was dark for three days and there was widespread confusion with people running helter-skelter and currency notes flying around with no one interested in them. During the dream, she became aware that the earth had just entered the Photon Belt.

Our Channel Suvahini had the following vision of events taking place in the year 2018:

"Meditators are all meditating in a place. Others are screaming. There is a lot of fear and chaos outside but the Meditators are not disturbed by it. The Meditators have filled themselves with a lot of white Light. Earthquakes are happening outside. All those who are meditating have qualified and grown spiritually.

"They are channelling a lot of Light to help those who are suffering. About 80% of world's population that has not transformed is outside this place.

"Then Lord Kalki, the World Teacher, descends down to places where people are meditating and asks everyone to meditate for three days. He says, "Let us hold a lot of Light and let us start living on Pranas during this period. Many people who are outside will die and will be shifted to the seven earths to transform further."

"All Gods and Goddesses are descending down. They bring down a globe of Golden Light. Then Mahavatara (*see below*) fixes a pencil shaped gadget on everybody, which helps them to sustain good qualities. It helps to receive Prana directly from the Sun. It will also help us bring down rare knowledge to help others.

"Because of this pencil like gadget, people will all be of similar size and weight. All will be beautiful to look at also."

Mahavatara

The World Teacher, who is known by names like Maitreya, Lord Kalki etc. comes down to this earth to guide humanity during the transition to the New Age. Once the transition is complete and we enter the Light Age, life on earth is managed by the Rishis under the guidance of Mahavatara, who is an incarnation of Maha Vishnu. The western prophet Nostradamus knew about Him. Nostradamus called Him by the name 'Kiran'.

Mahavatara has taken birth and is ready and waiting to emerge.

Our Destiny

Much of what is in this book is about the events that are likely to take place in the near future. Regardless of the authenticity of such predictions, we can say that these are only the possibilities. Any future event, however strongly predicted, may or may not take place. This is because, our future depends on us. Humanity can work collectively and choose the kind of future it wants. All it needs is for the world to come together and work selflessly as one group with a single objective of reducing human suffering.

But we know that it is not easy to mobilise the entire humanity. What can we do as individuals about ourselves and the world?

The next section explains the ways and techniques that have the power to transform us and impact the world.

The Action Plan

Guruji Krishnananda

The Action Plan to sail through 2012 and live in the Photon Belt is simple. Unbelievably simple. It is to purify ourselves and transform to become truthful, peaceful and all-loving. It is to manifest our true nature of Love and Light.

This appears very simple but, we know, it is very difficult, particularly after having gone through 5000 years of darkness, Kali Yuga. But there is no choice. The Photon Belt spoke to our Special Channel Suvahini and said: "Change or perish."

Because it is difficult to change, the Rishis, Lord Kalki and Lord Maitreya, the Ruler of Shambala, and many many Light Workers, are waiting to help and guide us. One has to choose the life of Light. Then, one gets all help.

This is the time to choose. There is no more time to sit on the wall and wait.

There is no place for non-love, violence and corruption in the Photon Belt. It is full of Love, Peace and Light. To enter the Photon Belt and sail through 2012, I suggest, as a part of the Action plan, to practise the following technique daily. This technique can be practised by anyone and everyone. This is not a religious but Spiritual means.

The Technique:

Channelling the Light

Light is the Source from which all this creation has come. This Light is everywhere at a different frequency. It has

Intelligence, Love and Peace. When we channel Light, we transform ourselves and also the world.

I have initiated The Light Channels World Movement on 18-5-2008. For details, please visit www.lightchannels.com.

To channel the Light, sit comfortably facing North and imagine an ocean of Light above you. Imagine the Light entering you and filling up your entire body. Experience the Love and Peace of the Light for a moment and then imagine the Light spreading around you filling your home, locality, nation and the whole world gradually.

Practise this daily for 7 minutes.

You can also practise this technique for an hour and more. This is a kind of higher Meditation. Meditating for hours at a stretch will be required in future.

Other Techniques

There are other techniques which help establishing contact with the Photon Belt and other special energy fields. I feel that they have to be practised under personal guidance.

I feel Meditation of any Path helps and leads to the preparation to enter the New Age.

FINALLY ...

This small book is meant not to scare but to awaken. The world will not end in 2012. And there will be new beginnings.

List of our publications

Doorways to Light
Beyond 2012
Living in Light
Light
A Package from the Rishis
(containing 5 Booklets)
- How to Meditate
- Dhyana Yoga
- Descent of Soul
- Practising Shambala Principles
- Astral Ventures of a Modern Rishi

The Master Answers
Channelled Knowledge from the Rishis
Guruji Speaks Part-I
Guruji Speaks Part-II
The Book of Reflections-Vol-I
The Book of Reflections-Vol-II
New Age Realities
iGuruji Vol 1
iGuruji Vol 2
Living in the Light of My Guru
Meditators on Meditations
Meditators on Experience
Meditational Experiences
Awareness

ಬೆಳಕಿಗೆ ಬಾಗಿಲುಗಳು
ಬೆಳಕು
2012 - ಅಂತ್ಯ ಅಥವಾ ಆರಂಭ
2012 ನಂತರ
ಋಷಿಗಳಿಂದ ಬಂದ ಜ್ಞಾನ
ಐ–ಗುರೂಜಿ ಭಾಗ 1
ಐ–ಗುರೂಜಿ ಭಾಗ 2
ಅನಿಸಿಕೆಗಳು
ಋಷಿಗಳಿಂದ ಬಂದ ಕೊಡುಗೆ
(ಐದು ಪುಸ್ತಕಗಳು)
- ಧ್ಯಾನ ಮಾಡುವುದು ಹೇಗೆ
- ಧ್ಯಾನ ಯೋಗ
- ಆತ್ಮದ ಅವರೋಹಣ